The One Choice rule

The "One" Choice rule

Transform Your Life and Work by Changing Your Mindset and Behavior

Tracy Butz

TRACY BUTZ

The One Choice rule

Transform Your Life and Work by Changing Your Mindset and Behavior

Tracy Butz

Published by:
Lakeview Press
Thornton, Colorado

Printed in the United States of America

Cover design by Mike Heidl
Copy edited by Tani Grimh
Wisconsin

Library of Congress Control Number: 2018914426

ISBN: 978-0-9882207-7-5

CONTACT TRACY

To schedule Tracy to speak at your event, call:

920.450.2118

For more information, visit Tracy's website:

TracyButz.com

Dedication

I dedicate this book to those who continue to inspire me and enrich my life in endless ways.

First, to my husband—thank you for supporting and believing in me through every challenge and new idea. I am grateful for your words of encouragement when desired and your echoed excitement in times of celebration.

Second, to my boys—I am incredibly proud of the young men you've become. May you learn from your mistakes, walk with courage and purpose, and continue to live a life with integrity, love and happiness.

Third, to my readers, keynote audiences, workshop participants, and social media followers—you continue to amaze me with your stories, knowledge and insight. Thank you for sharing your experiences and for continuing to welcome my expressions of inspiration and influence. It is because of you that I can continue to enjoy my true passions.

Contents

Introduction

If a trusted authority figure said you needed to make several difficult and enduring changes in the way you think and act, and if you didn't your time would end soon, could you change when change really mattered? Yes, you say? Well, according to Dr. Ray Levey, founder of the Global Medical Forum, "The scientific odds are nine to one against you."

Consider a teenager, who suffers a drug overdose from synthetic marijuana, also known as K2 or spice. After being rushed by ambulance to the hospital, fighting for his life, all his family was able to do was stand aside helplessly and watch the team of doctors work to stabilize him. After several long and grueling hours, he was finally considered *out of the woods.* Later that evening, he was somewhat lucid and able to understand how close he came to facing a dreadfully avoidable demise.

After spending a week in the hospital, this young man was admitted to an area inpatient drug and alcohol treatment facility. This option failed. He was then admitted to an intensive outpatient drug and alcohol treatment program. This option failed. He was then admitted to a residential treatment facility across the state, where he lived and received both behavioral counseling and treatment for addiction. This option also failed.

Upon arriving back home and experiencing a forced withdrawal from high school—because that was where the overdose happened—his behavior became even more out of control. After continued and reckless drug use, endless bouts of couch-surfing, hanging in trap houses, running from police night after night, all while lying, stealing and completely defying all rules—his parents were at a loss for what to do. They were deeply troubled about how this erratic lifestyle the family was now living would affect each of them, and agonized over various suggested paths from professionals and countless well-intentioned friends. They finally made the arduous and painful choice to no longer allow their son to live with them, as long as his careless behavior continued.

To his parents' dismay, their son's rash behavior didn't slow. Over time, invitations to crash from his friends diminished, where he chose to then seek evening shelter in his car with the engine on, shivering with a barely working heater in below zero temperatures. Eating anything he could find—which included dumpster diving—and bathing where he could—whether it was at the local YMCA or even at the edge of a nearby pond on slightly warmer days—he became an emaciated form of himself.

Over time, as fate would have it, the police began to better understand his routine and habits. The cycle of being arrested, obtaining probation, breaking probation, having a warrant out for his arrest, and eventually wearing orange also became a pattern—coupled with limitless tears and an unthinkable number of broken promises.

He spent his 18th birthday behind bars.

He spent his 19th birthday behind bars.

He spent his 20th birthday behind bars.

The truth is, changing behavior is difficult. And just because you want behavior to change, it doesn't mean it will. Behavior change doesn't work that way. It certainly didn't for one young man I love dearly. And whether we face a daunting change we know we need to make ourselves, or we are desperately trying to persuade someone we care about to change a negative behavior that is holding him/her back, we know changing behavior isn't easy for anyone. The odds of making change happen are stacked high against us; yet, we are all confronted with it personally and professionally.

The exciting news is that in this book, you'll discover groundbreaking insight and tools for action to help you overcome the odds and successfully change behavior, *one choice* at a time.

Maybe your spouse works too many long hours and isn't there when you really need him/her, causing animosity and hardship for you and your family. Perhaps a candid conversation with a co-worker is needed due to her/him consistently challenging decisions, both those you make and choices framed by your team, negatively affecting relationships, productivity and performance results for all. Or possibly, you realize you need to make a lifestyle shift due to the increased amount and frequency you are choosing to hit the bottle, in an attempt to numb the unparalleled stress you are experiencing. It just may be time to ask yourself, "What one choice is standing before me, front and center, that if I choose to commit to it, I could positively and dramatically alter my life?"

Decide to better understand your spouse's perspective. Opt to engage in candid dialogue with a fellow colleague. Agree to decrease stress in your life, so the need to anesthetize will diminish. Once you make one conscious choice toward true behavior change, the ripple effect of ongoing positive change can occur, one choice after another.

In the chapters ahead, you'll learn *how* to apply The One Choice Rule to your life and work, influencing and inspiring you to foster behavior changes you want to make, as well as those you know you should make. Your decision to read this book and then take purposeful action, will certainly help position you toward positive change. Make today the day you choose to begin transforming your life by following The One Choice Rule: *One choice can change everything.*

Chapter 1

Progress Not Perfection

"Perfectionism is not a quest for the best. It is the pursuit of the worst in ourselves, the part that tells us that nothing we do will ever be good enough— that we should try harder." *Julia Cameron*

"You've been destined to live in victory, destined to overcome, destined to leave your mark on this generation." *Joel Osteen*

"Make the most of yourself....for that is all there is of you." *Ralph Waldo Emerson*

Progress Not Perfection

Often times, people avoid making changes in their life because they just don't know what steps to take. The process can seem overwhelming; they may feel they don't have the time or resources to get "there." And if where to start is unclear, either excuses are made or people become stuck and unable to take even one step forward. These realities occur when unrealistic expectations are set, and we believe that if we're not perfect in our pursuit we are a failure. The truth is, because we are human, we are unable to attain perfection. Being imperfect is what makes each of us unique. And that's a good thing.

Perfection should never be the goal because the outcome likely will be failure. This doesn't mean we don't set the bar high, because we absolutely should. But we need to focus on progress, not perfection; target the process we are experiencing now and the steps we are taking, not on the outcome being perfect.

So where should you start? In order to make a lasting change, the change itself needs to be meaningful to you. It can't feel imposed upon you, but rather is chosen by you. For example, let's say you want to spend more time reading interesting and insightful books. In order to carve out the necessary time in your schedule, you choose to reduce your

Facebook interaction time by two hours per week. If someone told you that you had to make that change, you probably wouldn't take kindly to that demand. Furthermore, if someone took it upon themselves to limit your Facebook involvement by two hours per week, you likely would loathe it more, primarily because it's a change being done to you. No one likes change forced on them. No one.

The truth is, changing behavior is difficult. And just because you want behavior to change, it doesn't mean it will. Behavior change doesn't work that way.

In addition to the change being meaningful to you, it also has to be something that you believe in, that you value, that you want to get behind and commit to. You have to know the work ahead of you will be worth it. So what habit or behavior are you wanting to change in your life, and why do you want to do it?

Do you want to go back to school and earn a diploma or degree?

Do you want to feel happier?

Do you want a job you enjoy?

Do you want to make more money?

Do you want to lose weight?

Do you want to find love?

Do you want to stop smoking?

Do you want to be more confident?

Do you want to say "no" more often?

Do you want to find your passion?

Do you want to laugh more?

Do you want to be a better spouse?

You are one decision away from totally transforming your life. Imagine that!?! And just know, I am with you on this journey, and I am a work in progress, too! I continue to make changes in my life, so I keep growing and propelling myself forward, becoming better and better. The question I ask myself before deciding to alter a habit or behavior is, "Will this one choice to change, help me get one step closer to becoming my greatest self?" If the answer is, "Yes," I know I am on the right track.

Aim for awesomeness. Strive for spectacular. And allow yourself some wiggle room for slips and trips.

Personal Challenge

What habit or behavior are you wanting to change in your life and why do you want to do it?

Will this one choice to change, help you get one step closer to becoming your greatest self?

Chapter 2

Trust *Your* Truth

"Being confident and believing in your own self-worth is necessary to achieving your potential." *Sheryl Sandberg*

"Using the power of decision gives you the capacity to get past any excuse to change any and every part of your life in an instant." *Tony Robbins*

"Good decisions come from experience, and experience comes from bad decisions." *Author Unknown*

Trust *Your* Truth

Once someone decides to make a specific choice, have you ever thought about why someone selects this choice over that choice, or this path instead of that path? I am totally fascinated with why people make the decisions they do. What steps did they take in their head, or was it a quick gut reaction without much thought? Also, after a decision is made, why do some people appear completely confident in their choice and others continue to waffle back and forth saying, "I should have done this, or I should have done that." Is it even possible to make decisions that we won't regret? The simple answer is, "Absolutely."

When we are faced with making a decision, the decision itself exists in the present and concerns the future. You will never know in advance whether a decision is the right one, simply because you can't see into the future.

However, let me ask you another question. At what point do you feel regret over a decision you made? It always occurs after you have made the decision. See, it's possible to feel regret only when you are looking back in time, after you've made your decision, after you've seen the outcome of your decision and, for some reason, you wish the outcome were different. So it wasn't the decision itself that bothered you.

Rather, the outcome of that decision is what you regret and wish were different.

The secret to confident decision-making lies in understanding the feelings and emotions that are likely going to influence your decision. Of all the variables in one's head when making decisions—your family's needs, your monetary constraints, concerns from your work colleagues— we are most certain of our own feelings. Yet, many people grow up learning to mistrust those feelings. "Don't be ridiculous," or "Don't feel that way," or "You should be/feel happy, grateful, relieved, etc.," are common responses we hear when demonstrating vulnerability and expressing our feelings. I don't understand why some people feel compelled to tell me how I should, or am, feeling.

When you're faced with a tough choice, remember to weigh your options closely, and then do your best to trust and feel confident in your decision.

Over the course of the last six months, our beloved 14-1/2-year-old miniature apricot poodle, Snickers, has been struggling with hip-related issues, significant arthritis, a 99 percent loss in hearing, and cataracts that severely limit his vision. Our veterinarian prescribed several medications that provided pain relief, until lately. Snickers' right leg is now slightly dragging when he walks, he is unable to sit up normally, he sometimes falls down the steps when going outside, is unable to walk up the stairs himself, and in the past several days, circles slowly round and round before finally being able to just lie down, squealing at times from pain. My husband and I have struggled with the decision of having him put down. It seems incredibly wrong to do that to a precious member of our family. Then my sister reminded me of a poem she has kept for many years after discovering it on Dear Abbey entitled, "The Last Battle:"

If it should be that I grow frail and weak,
And pain should keep me from my sleep,
Then will you do what must be done?
For this – the last battle – can't be won.
You will be sad I understand,
But don't let grief then stay your hands,
For on this day, more than the rest,
Your love and friendship must stand the test.

We have had so many happy years,
You wouldn't want me to suffer so,
When the time comes, please let me go.
Take me to where my needs they'll tend,
Only, stay with me until the end,
And hold me firm and speak to me,
Until my eyes no longer see.

I know in time you will agree,
It is a kindness you do for me.

Although my tail its last has waved,
From pain and suffering I have been saved.
Don't grieve that it must be you,
Who has to decide this thing you do.
We've been so close – we two – these years,
Don't let your heart hold any tears.

Author Unknown

Yesterday, Snickers and I snuggled together, relishing our strong bond as I held him tightly in my arms, trying to catch a few moments of restful sleep. As he lay his head on me, his kisses caressing my arm, he closed his eyes and whimpered ever-so-slightly. I knew at that moment the pain had to end. I had to make the incredibly tough decision to release him from his agonizing fight.

What I didn't want to hear is, "Don't feel sad;" yet, I did. How does another person decide they have the right to tell me how I should or shouldn't feel?

When a situation feels scary, it is. When you feel happy, you are. When a decision feels right to you, it is. These are your feelings; no one else's. Trust them. When you're faced with a tough choice, remember to weigh your options closely, and then do your best to trust and feel confident in your decision. Don't let someone else invalidate your feelings or cause you to question them.

When making decisions, know that setbacks happen, plans change, disappoints come, and losses occur. One thing I know for sure is that choosing to make no decision is a decision, too. Rather than mistrusting your feelings, and being paralyzed from your perceived lack of control, own the feelings as yours, and choose to make the best decision you can based on *your* truth. After all, only *you,* should and can judge *your* decision.

Personal Challenge

When contemplating your next difficult decision, consider what feelings and emotions could influence your decision-making process, weigh your options carefully, and then do your best to trust and feel confident in *your* decision.

Chapter 3

Cultivate What Matters

"People who climb to the top of just about any field eclipse their peers through something as basic as deliberate practice." *Joseph Grenny*

"We are what we repeatedly do. Excellence, then, is not an act, but a habit." *Aristotle*

"If we want to direct our lives, we must take control of our consistent actions. It's not what we do once in a while that shapes our lives, but what we do consistently." *Tony Robbins*

The **One** Choice rule

Cultivate What Matters

❖ ❖ ❖ ❖ ❖

Habits are powerful forces. They influence what our brain tells us to do, based on your decisions that have become engrained routine. Everyone has routines, or habits; things you just do—without thinking about them. According to research from Duke University, up to 45 percent of your actions are unconscious habits. This means that a significant part of what you think, say, feel and do are strongly shaped by your habits—whether they are positive or negative.

But all habits are not created equal. Some have little impact on your life, and others, referred to as "keystone habits," can affect your life immensely. Exercising on a regular basis is one example of a keystone habit—which is a habit that creates a domino effect on the rest of your life by naturally influencing you to build more breakthrough routines that produce positive outcomes. Keystone habits—a term originally coined by Charles Duhigg, a Pulitzer-prize winning American journalist and non-fiction author—are very different from regular habits, like posting a daily message on multiple social media platforms. A regular habit is a positive thing to do, but whether you choose to do it or skip it, it doesn't have a huge impact on the rest of your life. By contrast, a keystone habit, like consistently exercising five days per week, is a habit that can also lead to other positive, unintended outcomes like:

- Stronger and more flexible body
- Enhanced mood
- Decreased level of stress
- Reduced risk of heart disease
- Enhanced productivity
- Improved quality of sleep
- Heightened brain function

After developing a keystone habit, you're often filled with a sense of accomplishment, which offers a small win that you can then build upon. They provide motivation to engage in other good habits—like with exercise, you tend to drink more water and eat healthier. And keystone habits also tend to fill you with energy, confidence, and the momentum to achieve even more.

When you choose to make keystone habits a non-negotiable part of your routine, you change. You take more control of your life and the positive ripple effect naturally occurs. There are many keystone habits you can adopt and they are different for everyone. In addition to exercising consistently, here are several other common ones:

- **Active goal-setting.** Envision and outline specific goals annually, writing them on paper to help drive focus and commitment. Break down each goal into milestones that can be accomplished on a daily, weekly and/or monthly basis to enhance motivation and easily gauge results.

- **Invest in daily gratitude.** Appreciate what you already have. Even though it's hard to see what you have, as opposed to what you don't have, this habit is integral to a positive mind and a thankful heart.

- **Challenge yourself.** Rather than being complacent with the status quo, success in life comes from continuing to challenge yourself. Focus on rediscovering a forgotten passion, learn a new skill, explore another interest, or do something better today than you did yesterday.

- **Eat dinner together as a family.** Not only does this habit encourage healthier eating patterns—like a greater opportunity for portion control and nutritionally balanced meals—but it also is a perfect setting to expose your family to different foods, save money with less expensive home-cooked entrees, and spend quality time together. Moreover, according to a report by Court Appointed Special Advocates for Children (CASA), when this routine is practiced at least five times per week, a teen's chance of smoking, drinking, and using drugs is drastically decreased.

- **Make your bed.** It may seem irrelevant, but tidying up your bed as part of your morning routine is a small, quick habit that sets a precedent of order and productivity for the day. Creating a neat and organized environment can positively impact your mental state with a small sense of accomplishment—in just 30 seconds, no less.

- **Discard and replace.** Choose one day a week, or every other week, or even once a month, where you discard something you don't love or need. This process helps reduce clutter and gives you the opportunity to replace things that don't add value with items you enjoy and appreciate.

- **Continue learning.** Learning a new skill or language, or starting a project that has measurable goals, is a great way to boost your self-confidence, while also gifting you with invaluable knowledge. There are countless different things you can learn, depending on where your interests lie. Enrich your life, and reap the benefits.

- **Think and talk positively.** Rather than focusing on the famous lyric by award-winning singer and songwriter, Pink, which says, "Change the voices in your head; make them like you instead," consciously focus every day on your positive attributes and what you do well. This isn't to say that you should have an inflated ego or not admit faults; just spend much more time directing your thoughts and inner voice toward happy views of yourself. Heck, every morning when you look in the mirror, smile and recite actor Billy Crystal's famous line, *"You look mahvelous!"*

- **Save more money.** By saving [more] money you will have emergency funds for the unforeseen. This can often lead to a more money-conscious lifestyle for you and your family. By saving money you'll pay closer attention to the trivial purchases you're making, and feel the confidence of being insulated financially against the unexpected.

- **Sleep more.** Along with nutrition and exercise, getting an adequate amount of sleep is one of the pillars of good health; yet, today, people are sleeping less than ever before. Their sleep quality has decreased as well. Sleep improves concentration and productivity. Getting a good night's sleep is incredibly important for your health.

- **Efficiently manage time.** Because every person has exactly the same amount of time per day, this habit represents a great equalizer. Rather than engaging in distractions and time-wasting activities, spend your time wisely, focused on the tasks at hand.

- **Exercise consistently.** Exercise is quite possibly one of the most beneficial keystone habits, as it helps to energize the body, clear the mind, and rejuvenate the spirit. It improves health and diminishes the chances for disease, while increasing your motivation to achieve more.

The development of keystone habits is a powerful technique to help you literally transform your life, and it's actually quite easy to implement them. Start by making a list of habits you would like to develop and incorporate into your life over the next 12 months. After you have created a list, note next to each habit why it is important to you. This process helps you to clearly see the benefit of doing each one. Then for each habit, determine if it is a keystone habit by writing "yes" or "no" in that applicable column. Remember, if it is a keystone habit, it will have other positive unintended results. Then for those habits where you have answered "yes," capture potential positive unintended outcomes that could occur from incorporating that habit into your routine.

When you choose to make keystone habits a non-negotiable part of your routine, you change. You take more control of your life and the positive ripple effect naturally occurs.

Next, outline what actions you would need to take for that habit to become routine. For example, if you want to develop the keystone habit of sleeping eight hours every night, what would it take to make that habit a reality? You may need to eat dinner a bit earlier to avoid digestive issues occurring, or build 15-30 minutes of relaxation or reading into your bedtime routine to make it easier to fall asleep, or you may need to set your alarm for 30 minutes later in the morning and cut out some unnecessary tasks you currently do before heading to work.

After outlining the necessary actions for each keystone habit, prioritize which one keystone habit to tackle first. Consider which one is most important to you and what you want to accomplish. Weigh the benefit(s) and think through what you currently have going on in your life, and if you can realistically take the necessary actions to make this particular habit integral in your routine. Remember, you can always talk yourself into why it isn't a good time to make a change right now; so don't use the excuse of being too busy or your life being too chaotic to begin implementing any of them. If you want to see positive change in your life, you must commit to doing some work to make it happen. Like the famous saying goes, "If you always do what you've always done, you'll always get what you've always got."

Lastly, for the keystone habit that is highlighted as priority one, write down feasible completion dates for each of the actions you need to take for that habit to come to fruition, noting the final anticipated completion date that specific habit will be incorporated into your life. Here is an example of how a plan could begin to take shape:

Desired Habit	Why Important to Me	Keystone Habit — Yes/No	Potential Unintended Results for "Yes'" only	Actions for Keystone Habit to Become Routine	Prioritize Keystone Habits	End Dates per Action	Final End Date
Exercise five days/wk	Assist in better controlling weight	Yes	Stronger, more flexible body; Healthier food choices; Reduced risk of heart disease; Improved quality of sleep	Set aside 30 min. to exercise five days/week Hire treadmill tech. to ensure it works properly Ask husband to prepare dinner three days/week	1	W date X date Y date	Z date
Sleep eight hours every night	Need to operate at the highest level of productivity	Yes	Enhanced attention span; Greater ability to remember; Feel more rested and better overall	Eat dinner earlier—avoid digestive issues; Build 15-30 min. of relaxation into bedtime routine; Set alarm 30 min. later in morning to cut out needless tasks before work.	2		
Drink one vs. two cans soda per day	Decrease amount of sugar consumed	No	N/A	N/A	N/A	N/A	N/A
Save $100 more/mth	More money available for unexpected expenses	Yes	Reduces anxiety; More financial freedom; Enhanced financial awareness; Increased flexibility with monetary purchases	Track what we spend money on today; Create and follow a budget that aligns with our goals Ensure $50/check is automatically transferred to savings	3		

Rather than going through life without thoughtful intention, make today the day you choose to cultivate one keystone habit. By taking this one small action, you will likely find the momentum to set off a slow avalanche of additional changes, positively transforming your life in amazing ways. The One Choice Rule: one choice can change *everything*.

Personal Challenge

Identify which keystone habit you commit to adopting in the next 30 days to move you one step closer to transforming your life. Then answer these questions related to that habit:

- Why is this habit important to me?
- What are some potential unintended results?
- What actions must be taken to have it become a routine?
- What are the anticipated completion dates for each action item?
- When do I think this keystone habit will be fully integrated into my routine?

Chapter 4

Kick 'Em to the Curb

"The pessimist sees difficulty in every opportunity. The optimist sees the opportunity in every difficulty." *Winston Churchill*

"Change does not occur by merely willing it any more than behavior changes simply through insight." *Leo Buscaglia*

"The secret to permanently breaking any bad habit is to love something greater than the habit." *Bryant McGill*

The **One** Choice rule

Kick 'Em to the Curb

I t's 3 p.m., and you're knee-deep in an afternoon energy slump. You decide it's time for a quick pick-me-up and grab a can of diet soda. As you pop it open and start swigging a few gulps back, your eyes become laser-focused on the candy dish, located on the counter to your right, filled with the usual bite-sized white chocolate Reese's Peanut Butter Cups…your treasured tasty treat!

Grabbing one and eagerly unwrapping it, you make the bold choice of "one-and-done," and down the hatch it goes. And because you barely tasted it, and they're so tiny after all, you snatch another and do the "two-bite-shuffle"—enjoying the perfect balance of peanut butter and white chocolate in each equally-sized indulgence. Yummy! Without even thinking, you quickly reach for a third, feverishly pulling back the foil and then tapping the breaks to slowly start "stripping-the-gear"—nibbling around the edge to carefully remove the dense chocolate ridges, and leave a delectable circle of peanut butter filling with a thin chocolate coating. As a serious candy connoisseur and diehard peanut butter fan, you revel in the fact that the third time's a charm, since that method allowed you to experience the highest peanut butter–to-chocolate ratio. There may be *no wrong way to eat a Reese's,* but there certainly is a right way.

As a smart, ambitious person, you know bad habits can keep you from reaching your goals and can even negatively transform your life—opposite of keystone habits. You also know you're capable of self-control; yet, despite your best efforts, you've been unable to change. Whether it's mid-day snacking, procrastinating, or skipping workouts, feeling powerless in the face of bad habits can really take a toll on your motivation, and even with your self-esteem. What if it's not a lack of willpower that's to blame? What if the advice you've been given about how to "break" a bad habit is actually misguided? If you've been trying different methods over and over again, but nothing's working, it's time for a new approach that leverages the science of behavior change.

Habits are described as having three distinct stages: cue, routine, reward. In the above example, fatigue was the *cue,* also known as a trigger. My fatigue triggered a *routine,* which was to get a soda. My *reward* was delighting in blissful confection perfection—that provided a temporary energy boost, too.

The habit loop, as it's referred to, is incredibly powerful. It is hardwired into our psyches, which explains why habits are so hard to "break." We actually never *break* bad habits; we replace undesired behaviors with more positive alternatives.

If you're wanting to kick a bad habit to the curb, here's three easy steps for leveraging the habit loop to finally change your behavior. The steps are easy to understand, but as you can imagine, they can be hard to work through.

Step 1: Identify the stages. Identify the cue, routine and reward that led to your habit. Look at the circumstances surrounding the behavior—like the time of day, where you are, who you're with, how you feel, etc. For example, recognize how after experiencing a heated argument with your daughter (cue), you plop down on the couch with a beer or glass of wine in one hand and your iPad in your other—ignoring your spouse (routine), as you push play on your go-to Netflix binge of the month, *Shameless,* openly relishing the epitome of family dysfunction, which helps you feel better about yours (reward).

Step 2: Explore alternatives. Explore healthier routines that can produce the results you want. Consider other behaviors that might provide a comparable reward to the one you are trying to eliminate. What else would give you a sense of accomplishment, enjoyment, happiness, relaxation, stress-reduction, avoidance, mental escape—whatever core need your current bad habit is satisfying? Could you swap out screen time with your favorite beverage, while ignoring your spouse, and instead take a relaxing walk, maybe invite your spouse and talk about the argument to help dissipate some of your stress?

Step 3: Commit to change. Now is the time to commit to altering your current routine with one of the new ones you've contemplated. And *commitment* is the key. Ask yourself, "On a scale of 0 to 10, how committed are you to making this behavior change?" Unfortunately, if you answer with anything other than a 10, the chances of you ever making that change aren't too likely. See, with commitment, you are either a 0 or a 10; nothing in between. You can't be partially committed; it's impossible. You're either committed—willing to do what it takes—or you're not. It's that simple. It's not easy; but it's simple.

You can't be partially committed; it's impossible. You're either committed— willing to do what it takes—or you're not. It's that simple.

Because changing behavior is hard, and sometimes even with your greatest effort, the change doesn't stick, revisit step two and consider trying another alternative behavior. Do your absolute best to not revert to your old ways out of sheer comfort. Research shows that as you continue to perform the same behavior in the same way, you develop strong neural pathways in the brain. What you did before becomes the path of least resistance. It is easier to keep doing what you have been doing than to change your behavior. This is not to say you cannot change, but just know that the longer you have been doing something, the more inclined you are to keep doing it.

If the bad habit you are trying to change is one you've had for a long time, anticipate and plan for setbacks. For example, if you are trying to lose some weight, think through situations that might challenge your newly defined eating habits—such as business dinners, upcoming holidays or special functions, traveling for work, or potential impending stressful events—and put a plan into place that guards against a slip-up. Perhaps you can read through the restaurant menu online ahead of time and pre-select a healthy meal choice to avoid the imminent temptation; or maybe you can eat a small healthy meal beforehand so as not to overeat, and then just slightly pick at the restaurant meal, enjoying the healthier components like vegetables.

I have found that if I work *within* the psychology of habits, rather than *against* it, I'm able to more successfully change my habits and alter unwanted, negative behaviors long-term.

Personal Challenge

What bad habit have you been wanting to "kick to the curb?"

1. Identify the cue, routine and reward that led to this habit.
2. Explore healthier routines that can produce the results you want.
3. What new routine will you commit to implementing to replace your current bad habit?

Chapter 5

Master Your Mindset

"You are imperfect, you are wired for struggle, but you are worthy of love and belonging." *Dr. Brené Brown*

"Until you are happy with who you are, you will never be happy because of what you have." *Zig Ziglar*

"What lies behind us and what lies ahead of us are tiny matters compared to what lives within us." *Henry David Thoreau*

Master Your Mindset

As you do your best to make the best choices and avoid negative habits from becoming ingrained as routine, do you ever find yourself wondering where you are on the path to your success? Are you close to reaching your true potential, or perhaps, are you stuck along the way? One question you may want to consider is if you have the right mindset to achieve the level of success you desire.

Mindsets are described as attitudes or beliefs that position the way you handle situations—meaning your conscious mental orientation, reactions and tendencies. Essentially, they help you sort out what is going on and what you should do next, within a set of circumstances. And when your mindset becomes habitual, it often defines not only who you are, but also who you can become.

Let's compare two common mindsets—fixed and growth. If you have more of a fixed mindset, you view your ability as innate, which makes failure very unsettling because it causes you to doubt how good you are. Those with a fixed mindset tend to avoid challenges, give up easily when faced with obstacles, see effort as pointless, ignore useful constructive feedback, and often feel threatened by the success of others—which, in turn, results in achieving less than their full potential.

By contrast, if you have a more growth-oriented mindset, you expect that you can improve your ability, and failure simply illustrates which aspects could be improved. When a challenge is encountered, those with a growth mindset usually embrace it and persevere in the face of setbacks. They see effort as a path to mastering a skill, focus on learning from feedback received, and look for inspiration in the success of others—which results in reaching even higher-than-expected levels of achievement.

Clearly, mindsets can dramatically affect our behavior and how we shape our lives. They influence our relationship with success and failure in both professional and personal contexts, and they can help or hinder us in reaching our full potential. My mindset in the past had a tremendous amount to do with learning to "not hate" myself because of what I saw on the scale.

Throughout my life, I have struggled immensely with maintaining my desired weight. Many years ago, I referred to my body image as a love/hate relationship…which is quite sad. The number I saw on the "cold, white analog-displayed body distortion box" every morning set the stage for the rest of my day. If the number was lower than I expected, I loved it, and it was going to be a super awesome day! If it came in at the number I anticipated, well, I guess things are okay. And if it came in higher than I was comfortable seeing, I absolutely hated it, and the plan for my day took a dramatic and depressing shift. I knew that perspective was neither normal nor healthy—as I can now openly discuss after countless sessions of counseling.

Today, I do my best to live my life in a healthy way, and keep my weight within a desired range. I no longer weigh myself daily and proudly have a much more positive relationship with food and my body image. I know I am not alone in this battle; yet, for those who have never struggled with this type of issue, reading these words have likely caused you pause. I get that. My point in sharing this intimate story with you, is that I struggle with real life issues like everyone else. All I can hope for is that a story I share or a point I make resonates at some level, and in some small way helps someone move through and eventually past it.

Mindsets can dramatically affect our behavior and how we shape our lives. They influence our success and failure, and they also help or hinder us in reaching our full potential.

So what if you want to alter your mindset—to view circumstances in your life more optimistically, and propel positive changes that foster greater levels of success and happiness? Viewing life through an optimistic lens is what I consider the *magic elixir*. Without it, you target the tumultuous. With it, you focus on the fantastic. Here are 10 strategies you can apply to immediately begin moving one step closer to *mastering your mindset:*

1. **Believe that you already are what you hope to be.** View yourself as already being successful in the role, profession or ability you desire. For example, if you want to be a more successful teacher, truly believe you are already an effective and thriving teacher, imparting wisdom and empowering your students to be their best. When you believe you are successful, you act and carry yourself as if you are.

2. **Identify role models you admire.** Choose several individuals who exemplify what you want for your life. Why do you admire them? What do they do that sets them apart?

3. **Create a personal vision statement.** Identify a vision of where you want to go and what barriers may be standing in your way. Describe your end result clearly, so you can see it.

4. **Break your vision into goals.** Write down specific goals that move you toward attaining your vision. Then prioritize your goals, focusing on only one or two at a time, so you are more likely to achieve them.

5. **Examine your social circle.** Do you socialize with individuals who reflect the values you have and support your dreams and goals? If not, it may be time to widen your circle. Networking or social events that have a positive purpose may be a good place to start.

6. **Challenge self-talk.** When you go to a store, do these words sound familiar: "Everything is too expensive!"? Reflecting on that statement, are all of the items priced too high, or is it that you only have so much money to spend there? When you are driving to work, do you often say, "People around here drive way too slow!"? As you weigh those words against the evidence, do they crumble under scrutiny because of your lack of patience, or do most drivers really meander far below the speed limit?

7. **Consume positive media.** Rather than watching programming about crime, violence or divisive politics, enjoy a media outlet that emphasizes a positive message. You can't change the news; but you can change what you watch or listen to.

8. **Volunteer to help those in need.** Offering a helping hand to those less fortunate can make a huge impact on how you feel about yourself and your view of the world. Yes, there are people in dire need; by volunteering your time and energy, you make a difference—which meets one of the most powerful intrinsic needs human beings have.

9. **Offer a gift of gratitude.** A simple gesture of genuine gratitude, like mailing a thank you note, can be very empowering. Not only does it feel good to the person sending it, but a thoughtful action creates goodwill in other people. As a bonus, demonstrating

gratitude can also strengthen relationships and personalize connections, especially since feeling appreciated is a universal need.

10. **Create a morning mindset routine.** Start every day by making a list of those things you are looking forward to over the next 12-15 hours. This list creates a feeling of anticipation and excitement that creates momentum for the entire day.

Every person has their own definition of success and happiness. If you want to achieve the level of each that you desire, altering your mindset may be *the one choice* to help position you best. If you expect the worst, you set yourself up to receive the worst. If you plan for and expect the best, you are one step closer to attaining it. Whether it is considered a magic mixture or a positive potion, mastering your mindset can propel your life forward in incredibly meaningful ways.

Personal Challenge

Of the 10 strategies outlined in this chapter, which ones will you apply immediately to help move you one step closer to mastering your mindset?

Chapter 6

Commit to Courage

"You learn more from failure than from success. Don't let it stop you. Failure builds character." *Unknown*

"We may encounter many defeats, but we must not be defeated." *Maya Angelou*

"Courage starts with showing up and letting ourselves be seen." *Dr. Brené Brown*

Commit to Courage

C ourage is considered by many to be one of the most important human virtues; yet, often times, many choose fear or comfort, over courage. And since we aren't born courageous, we shouldn't expect to miraculously acquire it without practice. In addition to exercising a positive mindset, courage is a muscle you must practice flexing if you want to display it more easily, which some professions realize and strive very hard to develop courage in their teams.

Whether it is a soldier fighting for his country on the front lines, a police officer who risks her life to save a civilian in a hostage situation, or a firefighter who rushes into a burning building to rescue someone trapped, these heroic actions define courage. Each one of these individuals stepped out of their comfort zone, dug deep, and mustered up the nerve and willingness necessary to place themselves in a situation where the outcome was unknown.

But since most of us don't work in a profession that demands daily demonstrations of unrivaled bravery, let's explore how you can learn to become more courageous. I'll first explain what courage is and is not, and then I'll share exercises you can practice at work or at home so you can perform small, daily acts of courage more often.

Courage is defined not as the absence of fear; but as being afraid and acting anyway. And when you think of courage you may picture physical bravery, but there are other forms of courage—ranging from physical strength and endurance to mental stamina and innovation. History highlights social activists, such as Rosa Parks and Nelson Mandela, as two individuals who chose to speak out against injustice at great personal risk. Entrepreneurs such as Steve Jobs and Walt Disney, took huge financial risks to follow their dreams and innovate, exemplifying the rewards courage can bring.

But sometimes, each of us comes face-to-face with this choice: courage or comfort? You can choose courage or you can choose comfort, but you can't choose both. They are mutually exclusive.

Over the years, my husband and I have been very blessed and fortunate enough to have taken breathtaking vacations that included exquisitely pristine, white–sand beaches caressed by crystal-clear turquoise seas, luxurious suites with unlimited lavish amenities, and all-inclusive gourmet dining havens—truly quintessential settings for romance, relaxation and even adventure—if that was of interest. With neither of us being adrenaline junkies who revel in thrill-seeking adventures, we rarely venture off a resort to partake in audacious excursions. However, at Secrets Maroma Beach Riviera Cancun Mexican Resort, we decided to step out of our comfort zone…just a bit.

Having no experience with zip lining—I timidly stepped off the landing and zzzip, I was flying over treetops and through the jungle at 60+ mph on a steel wire, fastened to a pulley using a security belt. Hanging on for dear life with a white-knuckle grip and eyes bulging out of my skull, the exhilarating feeling of flying like a bird—at mock speed, of course—was incredibly exciting and terrifying at the same time. As I approached the end of the line, I could barely see the stop mechanism, but was soon alarmed to learn that it was just a small block of cement or wood, adhered to the line with none-other-than *duct tape.* Seriously? In a split second, thoughts ran through my mind like, "That tiny block is designed to stop me from crashing into the landing affixed to that tower?" and "When I blow through that thing—where duct tape was trusted to create an unbreakable bond—will I fall to my death?" and "Why did we leave our safe and comfortable resort to do something so incredibly daring, scary and stupid?"

Courage is not the absence of fear; it's about being afraid and acting anyway. If you want to experience new things, demonstrating courage is often a necessary component.

As mentioned earlier, courage is not the absence of fear; it's about being afraid and acting anyway. If you want to experience new things, demonstrating courage is often a necessary component. Trying something you've not done before, is likely uncomfortable and sometimes, downright petrifying. But how do you know if you'll like something if you don't try it? As both freeing and frightening as this zip lining experience was for me, I determined that this is one adventurous activity I love! In fact, I recently zip-lined on the longest and also the fastest lines in all of Colorado! Exhilarating. Amazing. Mesmerizing. But whether it is zip lining, throwing your hat in the ring for a leadership role, or stepping up and having a tough conversation with someone, choices like these require courage.

Perhaps you are confronted with taking a chance when others will not, or your idea is very unpopular. Maybe you desperately want to follow your vision, no matter where it takes you, but you are meeting intense resistance. Perchance you are simply trying to do the right thing, even though far easier options exist. Most of us are called to be courageous more than we think, and we likely already possess many of the qualities that other remarkably courageous people have demonstrated. But if building definition in your courage muscle is a strength-enhancing exercise you want or need to target, highlighted below are 12 ways to grow that muscle:

1. **Stop procrastinating and give courage a try.** Do your best. Learn from the results of that first attempt and avoid becoming discouraged.

2. **Face what you fear.** Look it in the eye and determine exactly what you are afraid of. Rejection?

Being laughed at? Not being accepted? Then once you know what you fear, face it and tell yourself, "This fear will pass." Take one small step, then another. Action builds courage.

3. **Step outside your comfort zone.** By being open to meeting new people, visiting a city you have never been to but are curious about, or tasting an appealing entrée, one that you hadn't considered before, you gradually strengthen your ability to be courageous.

4. **Stand up for others who need it.** Find your inner strength to take a stand when necessary. Start by demonstrating courage when someone else is in need, rather than standing up for yourself first, since that is often times less intimidating.

5. **Demonstrate self-discipline.** Be very clear about what you want and don't want, and remain steadfast even when you are enticed to veer off course.

6. **Write an entry in a journal every time you do something you're scared to do.** You'll start to realize that you do brave things with some frequency. You're already much braver than you think.

7. **Find courage in numbers.** It's usually much easier initially to act in the company of others than dissenting solo.

8. **Find role models of quietly courageous people.** When you're trying to stretch yourself beyond your apparent limits, there's a part of you that likely wonders whether it can actually be done. A role model is a constant reminder that it can.

9. **Avoid self-doubt.** Rather than over-analyzing whether or not you can act courageously, leave your lack of self-confidence in the rear-view mirror and push forward.

10. **Lean into risk and uncertainty.** Conquer your fears by learning to deal with life's uncertainties. If you fear losing a huge account, figure out what it takes to keep it. If you fear becoming ill with cancer because of family history, be ruthless about annual check-ups, precautions, and pre-screening exams.

11. **Don't hesitate.** The more time your brain has to come up with excuses for not being courageous, the more time you will have to panic about hypothetical negative outcomes.

12. **Be willing to fail.** True learning happens when things don't go your way; when you fail or lose. Be willing to fail, but never willing to quit. Failure doesn't feel good, but the result, if you learn from it, is powerful.

Rather than succumbing to the learned behavior of fearfulness, know your limits, but commit to exercising courage more. If you want to transform your life and not reach the *end of your line* with regrets, make courage a conscious virtue you need to live with, versus without.

Personal Challenge

What is one skill you want to learn or one thing you are interested in trying?

What's holding you back from doing it? If fear is one of the reasons, what specifically are you afraid of?

If you want or need to demonstrate more courage in your life, which strategy highlighted in this chapter are you willing to try first?

Chapter 7

Strength Through Setbacks

"When life knocks you down, try to land on your back. Because if you can look up you can get up. Let your reason get you back up." *Les Brown*

"Sometimes life hits you in the head with a brick. Don't lose faith." *Steve Jobs*

"When tragedy occurs, it presents a choice. You can give into the void, the emptiness that fills your heart, your lungs, constricts your ability to think or even breathe. Or you can try to find meaning." *Sheryl Sandberg*

Strength Through Setbacks

As you strive to be courageous when facing adversity, have you ever wondered why some people seem to remain calm, while others appear to come undone? People who are able to keep their cool more effectively are known to be "resilient," or more able to cope with problems, challenges and setbacks.

Whether the issues include job loss, financial problems, illness, natural disasters, medical emergencies, divorce, the death of a loved one, or something else equally difficult, resilient people are more able to move through them. Instead of falling into despair or hiding from problems with unhealthy coping strategies, resilient people face life's difficulties head on. This doesn't mean they experience less distress, grief, or anxiety than other people; it means they handle those difficulties in ways that foster strength and growth. And in many cases, they emerge even stronger than they were before.

Resilience does not eliminate stress or erase life's difficulties. People who possess a high degree of resilience don't see life through rose-colored lenses. They understand that setbacks happen, and that sometimes life is hard and painful. They still experience the emotional pain, grief, and sense of loss that comes after a tragedy, but their mental outlook allows them to work through such feelings and recover, and potentially even prosper.

Research has shown that while some seem to come by resilience naturally, these behaviors can also be learned. Below are several strategies to help strengthen your resilience:

- **Nurture a positive view of yourself.** Remind yourself of your strengths and accomplishments. Self-esteem plays an important role in coping with stress and recovering from difficult events.

- **Develop a strong social network.** Having caring, supportive people around you helps you to share your feelings, gain support and perspective, and more easily walk away from the negative Nancy's and the pessimistic Paul's.

- **Be more accepting of change.** Not many things are permanent, and therefore change must come. And if you focus on how to change the things you cannot accept, it may be easier to accept the things you cannot change.

- **Take steps to solve problems.** Rather than wait for a problem to simply vanish, understand the scope of it, consider possible options, weigh the pros and cons of each, and move toward a successful solution by taking decisive action.

- **Take care of yourself. Pay attention to your own needs and feelings.** Make time for activities you enjoy, like spending time with a close friend or treating yourself to a relaxing massage.

- **Maintain a hopeful outlook.** Understand that a setback will pass, and expect that good things will happen again in your life soon. Cherish even the smallest successes, as those will help move you forward through the hardships.

- **Ask for help.** It is essential to ask for help during times of crisis or significant challenges. Ask for and accept assistance from trusted family, friends, support groups, and qualified professionals.

Realize you can positively move forward in times of adversity when you surround yourself with supportive and helpful people. Choose to take decisive action on things you can change. And remain hopeful, strong and determined always to persevere.

When I think of resilient people I know, I am reminded of a girl who experienced a life-changing event and how she chose to deal with it.

This girl, in her late twenties, was focused on climbing the corporate ladder. She had received three promotions already, but wanted more. She couldn't get from point A to point B fast enough. Life was all about being successful, along with an attractive salary and an evolving luxurious lifestyle. She knew all she had to do was push harder and she would achieve her towering goals.

Her parents and friends alike would even comment how amazed they were at what she could accomplish in one day. She frequently heard, "You do more in one day than I do in a week." Those comments energized her.

On a cool spring evening, she awoke to an achy feeling in her right elbow. She thought she must have slept on it wrong. Feeling exhausted, she fell asleep only to awake again, three hours later, now with pulsing pain in both elbows. Because it was almost time to get up, she decided to drag herself out of bed. Concerned, but knowing what her more-than-full schedule demanded of her that day, she chose to put her worries aside and move forward.

Over the course of the next several days, the pain began to intensify and spread. She now felt discomfort in her knees, ankles and wrists. It was time to see her family doctor, who referred her to a specialist. After numerous agonizing days awaiting the test results, she was stunned to hear the diagnosis. She was told she had Lupus—Systemic Lupus, to be exact.

Lupus is an autoimmune disease that can affect various parts of the body, including the skin, joints, heart, lungs, blood, kidneys and brain. Normally the body's immune system makes proteins to protect against viruses, bacteria, and other foreign materials. In an autoimmune disorder like Lupus, the immune system cannot tell the difference between foreign substances and its own cells and tissues, causing inflammation, severe pain, and damage in various parts of the body. Many people who have this disease live shortened lives, often caused by organ failure. She learned that 50 percent of those diagnosed usually end up on dialysis due to kidney failure. She was told her life going forward would now be different—and there was no cure.

Her doctor said firmly, "Make changes in your life, or Lupus will make them for you."

Realize you can move forward in times of adversity when you surround yourself with supportive people. Choose to take action. And remain hopeful, strong and determined always to persevere.

Over the next two years, she struggled to slow down. She wanted to pursue that next high-profile project, reach for the next desired promotion, and chase that next dream on her path to success. Her body continued to weaken; she was thin and frail and easily fatigued. Work consumed her energy and what little remained went to her family. She had nothing left for herself. Her life was deteriorating before her eyes. Even though her mind wanted it, her body wasn't willing or able.

The inflammation was so bad that she could barely grasp a fork to eat with or a pen to write with. She was unable to close her hand tightly to make a fist. The fatigue was so draining that on a good day she slept ten hours, with most nights requiring twelve or more. The pain was so intense that she could barely walk some days because taking each step caused her to pause. The quality of her life was not what she had imagined nor hoped for, and change was vital. She had approached her fork in the road.

This girl's story that you just read…is *my* story. I knew I could either continue down the current path of destruction or choose a different, more positive one that could lead to a life with greater meaning, peace and enjoyment. I decided it was time to make the one critical choice of altering my course.

I slept when I was tired, to allow my body to fight this unforgiving disease. I ate nutritious meals when I was hungry, to give my body the nutrients it desperately needed. I exercised a minimum of five days per week as advised, which allowed my joints to remain limber. I took all of my prescribed medication each day and strictly avoided the sun, which was difficult because relaxing in the sunshine was one of my favorite pastimes. I took leisurely walks, relaxed more often, listened to birds sing, and even made time for self-reflection. I began to laugh aloud more and enjoy the small, fun-filled moments that each day brought. I even made the decision to change careers—to focus all of my efforts toward my passions and what brought me happiness, rather than toward prestige and wealth.

Interestingly, once I chose to live all aspects of life in the present, doing what I enjoy, I began to genuinely live and appreciate life. In fact, the exact month I changed careers, my Lupus went into remission. The doctor said it likely wouldn't last long, so I should enjoy it. Well, 17 years have passed, and I am incredibly proud and happy to say that I am *still* in remission.

When you face unyielding adversity in your life, realize you can positively move forward when you surround yourself with supportive and helpful people, choose to take decisive action on things you can change, and remain hopeful, strong, and determined always to persevere.

When I heard I had Lupus, I had a choice to make. One option was to wallow in denial, look for pity, think and act as a victim, and make little-to-no changes in my life. Instead, I chose another option. I followed *The One Choice Rule* and chose to look at this disease as a gift. Had I not become ill with Lupus, I likely never would have slowed down to have my youngest son. Had I not been diagnosed with this disease, I would have never understood how wonderful and meaningful a family's love and support could be. Had I not been given the unwelcomed news of this ailment, I would have never learned to enjoy the art of landscaping, which happens to be one of my favorite hobbies today. Had I not been detected with this disorder, I wouldn't know how to relax, whether on a sandy beach or my living room couch. Had I not struggled to hear I had Lupus, I would never have felt compelled to share this story, or become a speaker and author with a desire to help others avoid a similar struggle, or inspire others with feelings of lasting hope and optimism, unwavering strength and resilience, and heartfelt support and love. This one choice I made...*changed everything.*

Personal Challenge

Consider a recent setback you faced in your life. What was it and how did it affect you and your life?

On a scale of 1 to 10 (low to high), how would you rate your level of resilience with that setback?

If you are interested in enhancing your level of resilience, what strategies will you practice?

Chapter 8

Alter Your Story

"You must stick to your conviction, but be ready to abandon your assumptions." *Denis Waitley*

"The harder you fight to hold on to specific assumptions, the more likely there's gold in letting go of them." *John Seely Brown*

"We simply assume that the way we see things is the way they really are or the way they should be. And our attitudes and behaviors grow out of these assumptions." *Stephen R. Covey*

Alter Your Story

So far you've read what powerful habits truly are and how to go about changing one. I've also shared the important concept of focusing on keystone habits and the huge impact they can have on your life. This chapter is devoted to altering one specific type of behavior...one that many people struggle with, even though they may be very resilient individuals.

Just because you want to or think you should change a behavior, knowing this point doesn't make it easy. Changing behavior takes more than a strong desire. Let's look at one behavior that many people want to better regulate or alter, which is better controlling their emotional reactions.

Human beings, we are reaction machines. And when it matters most, we often do our worst. So is it even possible to alter how we react in emotionally charged situations? The answer is "yes" and the solution is to *change the story* we tell ourselves. Let's examine the scenario below.

Paul is describing a new process improvement idea to his colleagues during his team's weekly meeting. As he is explaining the benefits of implementing this new software tool, he scans the room and notices one team member, Carla, who is clearly agitated—looking down, with her face starting to turn red, and her eyes beginning to somewhat bulge. Within moments, she begins to rock back and forth in her chair, then shifts her weight from side to side, and suddenly shouts out, "Are you serious? Do you think this software savior is going to fix all of the issues we are facing today? New technology will only take us so far; we need to listen to the ideas of our skilled workforce if we want to compete at the same level as our competitors! This is such a #$@&%* idea!" As she stormed out, the room immediately went silent. Heads around the table shifted down, with eye contact completely disappearing.

As I examine the facts of the situation, I acknowledge these points:

- Paul shared his new process improvement idea at the weekly team meeting.
- As he explained the benefits of the tool, he noticed Carla's face turning red and her eyes beginning to bulge, as she rocked back and forth in her chair, and then shifted her weight from side to side.
- Carla then began shouting about how the idea wouldn't work, used some vulgar language, and abruptly left the meeting room.

How would you characterize Carla's emotion? I describe it as angry or enraged. My guess is that you thought of or said a similar response. Given the facts, for Carla to exhibit anger or a similar emotion as she did, she likely assumed that Paul's idea wasn't an adequate solution; that it didn't include the opinions of the rest of the team, or perhaps it was an attempt to slide through a new piece of technology that Paul had wanted for the past year. Carla's interpretation of the situation led her to feel angry or enraged, where she then acted in a hostile manner.

> Rather than assuming the worst possible outcome and traveling down a self-defeating path, slow down your thought-process and consider interpreting the facts differently.

As you think about that less-than-ideal outcome, was there a different reaction Carla could have had? Instead of feeling anger or rage, is there a different emotion she could have experienced?

What if Carla felt an emotion on the opposite end of the spectrum from anger or rage—like feeling grateful for being part of a team that discusses new ideas and wants to hear the opinions of others before moving forward with a new idea? In order for an emotion like gratitude to emerge, Carla's interpretation of the facts, or the story she told herself, would have had to be very different. She could've viewed Paul's idea as a means of using a tool to supplement, rather than replace, the team's knowledge and experience to identify possible risks and consider viable solutions.

The second scenario certainly reveals a different story she told herself about the facts, which led her to experience a more positive emotion, altered her negative behavioral reaction to one that is much more pleasant, and led to an outcome which is far more favorable. Do you see how profound this concept is? The facts remain exactly the same. The only aspect that changes is the story, affecting the emotion that is felt, the natural behavioral reaction, with a corresponding outcome. If you want to impact your outcomes, start with the stories you tell yourself. If you can slow down your internal story-telling and consider a different and more positive one, imagine the outcomes you could experience when it matters most.

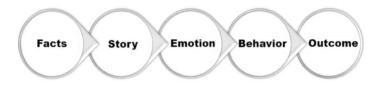

I'd like to put this concept into perspective on a personal level. It was the morning of April 5, 2005 and my dad called. I knew this call was different, because my dad has only initiated a phone call to me once before. Usually, my mom calls me or I call my parents' house. His voice was somber, soft and quiet. He searched for the right words, as he knew they would forever change my life. "Your mom," he said, "has a malignant brain tumor." Speechless for a moment, I asked him to repeat himself. He replied, "Unfortunately, you heard me right." My mom was too choked up to talk on the phone, so I told him I would be on the road shortly and get there as quickly as I could.

Because my biological dad lost his battle with cancer at the young age of 35 when I was only 4, the story I immediately told myself was that my mom was going to be a victim of a similar demise. This dreadful story, or assumption, led me to feel hopeless, helpless, angry and sad—literally consumed with despair.

As the tears poured down my face, I could feel the resentment inside of me start to build. I started to pace…back and forth, then back and forth again and again. I grabbed a suitcase and began disheveling the room, frantically thinking about what I needed to bring with me and what arrangements I needed to make—since I knew I would likely be gone for several days. As I slammed the door shut to my house, I jumped in my car, hit the gas out of my garage, and squealed the tires as I recklessly sped down the road—ignoring street signs and displaying a complete disregard for safety. Instead of arriving to my parents' house with a calm, supportive and loving demeanor, I charged through the front door in a frenzied, anxious and distraught state—clearly amplifying the distress instead of gently soothing it. The result of my behavior, which was fueled by the story I told myself, was less than ideal. Instead of helping the situation, I harmed it. At a time when my parents needed me most, I behaved my worst.

When you're presented with a set of unsettling facts, rather than assuming the worst possible outcome and traveling down a self-defeating and helpless path, slow down your thought process and consider interpreting those facts differently. Ask yourself, "Is there another story I could tell myself, one that may include an ounce of optimism?" After being told that my mom has brain cancer, instead of telling myself that she, too, was going to die from it, I could have altered my story by telling myself that many people today beat cancer; that a cancer diagnosis is not a death sentence. I would have then likely pondered what treatment options were available and what medical facility and doctors would represent the best option to treat her type of cancer. This story, versus the earlier one, would have most certainly led me to feel different emotions, causing me to behave in a more positive manner, resulting in a more calm and caring disposition upon arrival.

If you want to change how you emotionally react when faced with difficult circumstances, one choice I encourage you to make is to *alter your story.* This one choice can change *everything,* when it matters most.

Personal Challenge

Think through a time, preferably recently, where you behaved poorly, and it resulted in a less-than-ideal outcome. Consider each of the five components below and determine if you could've had a different outcome, had you altered your story.

1. What were the facts?
2. What story did you tell yourself about those facts?
3. What primary emotion of yours emerged?
4. How did you then behave?
5. What was the outcome?

Chapter 9

Positively Influence Change

"Everybody experiences far more than he understands. Yet it is experience, rather than understanding, that influences behavior." *Marshall McLuhan*

"Spend more time smiling than frowning and more time praising than criticizing." *Sir Richard Branson*

"Example is not the main thing in influencing others. It is the only thing." *Albert Schweitzer*

Positively Influence Change

In the introduction you read earlier, you learned of a truth, not a story, about a young man who I love dearly, whose behavior I desperately wanted to change. I realized I couldn't make him change, no matter how much I wanted to, because the only person's behavior I can definitely change is my own. Yet, one question I am asked often when I speak to groups is, "Can you influence someone to change?" My answer is always, "Yes, you certainly can."

The reality is, whether at work or at home, most people experience times when they need to influence others to think or behave differently. Perhaps you want a colleague to follow through on project expectations, or your spouse to not work so much, or a great friend to stop thinking and talking so negatively. If you find yourself faced with a task like this, here are five strategies I have used with great success to positively influence behavior change:

1. **Identify the specific behavior.** Pinpoint the exact behavior that you want this person to change. If you want the person to just "be less annoying" or "call more often," you will not get the results you want.

Pinpoint the exact behavior you want to change and note exactly how you want it to change.

- For example, rather than saying that you want her to "be less annoying," plan to say that you want her to "stop interrupting conversations she's not part of."
- Or, instead of wanting him to "call you more often," you could prepare to ask him to "call you every Sunday."

2. **Obtain and acknowledge perspective.** Determine what their concerns, fears and assumptions are regarding the change. Doing this will definitely help you counter some of their concerns, and you'll also better understand their perspective by valuing their opinion and incorporating them into the conversation. Even though you may not agree with their point of view, acknowledging that you understand and appreciate their perspective is a great way for you to confirm that you heard them and their point is valid.

3. **Explore motivations without pushing.** The other person often already knows that s/he should change a specific behavior. And if you try to present one side of an argument, s/he will feel compelled to push back. When trying to influence people who need motivation, but not more information, ask questions that allow them to explore their own motivations without feeling pushed. Some examples include:

- "What makes this behavior worth changing?"
- "If this change was easy, would you want to make it?"
- "What makes this behavior change hard?"
- "What are the pluses and minuses of changing or not changing?"
- "If you're able to successfully change this behavior, what would be different?"

4. **Highlight benefits for him/her.** Based on the individual motivations uncovered, subtly highlighting why changing could benefit this person can offer illuminated advantages that answer the question, "What's in it for me?" With this point in mind, laying out the advantages in this specific order also helps heighten the level of persuasion:

Essentially, you start out emphasizing a strong advantage and then bring closure by underlining the most important reason for him/her.

For example, my young adult sons are glued to their phones—texting, snap-chatting, watching videos, viewing or posting on Facebook, etc. Because I live in Colorado and they reside in Wisconsin, when we visit one another, spending quality time together is our shared focus. Sometimes, though, daily routines prevail and it becomes a bit more challenging to disconnect to reconnect. Since recommending a digital detox wouldn't work for them or me, I usually offer one or two reminders of how limited our time together is, and that's usually enough to re-engage them. Another option is to offer a source of inspiration like, "Let's go grab a bite and play some Topgolf," which almost always works.

But even only two or three years ago, things were different. Being young men in their late teens, boundaries were blurred and immaturity was elevated, so trying to enforce rules with limited leverage was tough. Here is how I drew attention to the behavior change I wanted to see, focusing on the benefits for them:

    a. No damaged relationships from rudeness and lack of interest — *second most important benefit*

    b. Won't decrease interaction and grow apart — *third most important benefit*

    c. You won't hear your Mom complain about it anymore — *first most important benefit*

5. **Address hidden influences.** Suppose a colleague at work, Patti, routinely arrives 10-15 minutes late for the weekly Tuesday 4pm team meeting, where your supervisor then spends the next 10 minutes reviewing what was already covered. This review causes the meeting to run over the allotted time, making you habitually late for your son's baseball game. After sharing your concern and reasoning with Patti, she

agrees that she needs to get to those meetings on time and that she will work hard to do that; however, there are influences that could hinder her success, such as:

- Her short-term motivation is directed by incoming client calls, questions from other team members, and a plethora of emails. Plus she has numerous distractions, like instant messaging, social media, and her cell phone.
- Rewards and punishments are aligned with other activities, like her performance goals are tied to client-service feedback, response time with addressing issues, etc.
- She has commented that she doesn't have a family that she needs to get home to in the evening, so she tends to work late often.

As you know, getting someone to make a commitment to change is not the same as getting them to actually change. But if you offer help in the right ways, that could positively tip the scale and provide the influence others need to change behavior. Perhaps in this situation you could consider:

- Demonstrating your commitment to helping Patti get to the weekly team meetings on time. Stop by her cubicle 10 minutes before the start time to kindly remind her and even offer to help her tie up any last-minute needs.

- Incorporating ground rules in meetings, with two rules being: to start and end meetings on time, and to no longer review information already covered for those who arrive tardy.
- Providing positive reinforcement when she makes it to a meeting on time, like words of appreciation and/or a thank you note.
- Suggesting to your supervisor that the department considers putting measurements and rewards in place to gauge and enhance productivity levels, including monitoring meetings that start and end on time.

Getting someone to make a commitment to change is not the same as getting them to actually change.

Everyone faces instances when positively influencing another person's thoughts or behavior is advantageous. Rather than impeding success, choose to offer assistance by understanding another's perspective, exploring their motivations and concealed influences, and encouraging commitment to change. When your intent to help is positive and genuine, your level of influence is endless and can truly make a difference. Now that is *one choice* worth making.

<u>Personal Challenge</u>

Whether in your professional or personal life, is there an individual you want or need to positively influence to think or behave differently?

If so, what strategy will you use to best position you for success?

Chapter 10

Dare to Live Fully

"Make your life a masterpiece; imagine no limitations on what you can be, have or do." *Brian Tracy*

"You cannot change your destination overnight, but you can change your direction overnight." *Jim Rohn*

"Instead of wondering when your next vacation is, maybe you should set up a life you don't need to escape from." *Seth Godin*

Dare to Live Fully

Some people measure success by the wealth they've accumulated, the power they've attained, or the status they've achieved; yet, even though they've reached success beyond their wildest dreams, they still have an empty feeling. They realize there is a huge void—something is missing from feeling fulfilled in their life—but, they don't know what it is.

Do you have a feeling or know someone who feels a sense of emptiness that can't be shaken? Take a few minutes today to reflect and consider, "Does what I'm doing matter?" "Am I living a life that is meaningful to me?" "Are my choices directing me toward living my best life?

Upon self-reflection, often times we aren't completely satisfied with where we are in our lives, yet we question making changes. Whether you want to influence a shift in yourself or another person, choosing indecision or deciding not to make a change is a significant risk. Rather than being risk-adverse, *dare* to step up to this challenge and confront it boldly. If you want to live a fuller, more purposeful and meaningful life, change must follow. And although everyone is different, there are common threads that bind a life with purpose, which include the following:

DARE TO BELIEVE IN YOU. Believe in yourself and your amazing talents. Realize you can do anything you put your mind to, but not everything.

DARE TO PURSUE YOUR PASSION. Passions provide true meaning and purpose in life. They energize and empower you. If you can't make your passion your career, make time for it every day.

No matter where you go and what you decide to do in life, dare to live fully. Every day, awake and make small daily enhancements, which over time, lead to transformative results. Dare to be your best you.

DARE TO BE BRILLIANT. Stretch your mind to learn, develop and expand. Invest the time and energy necessary to become your best.

DARE TO CONTRIBUTE. No matter what you do, you can bring something unique to the world. Contribute your value and gifts today.

DARE TO CONNECT. Connect with others in rich and meaningful ways. Be present, engaged and focused when interacting, not distracted and detached.

DARE TO LOVE. Dare to love with your whole heart. Love others deeply and let others love you completely.

DARE TO FORGIVE. Forgive by letting go and moving on. Nothing is more freeing than forgiveness. Free yourself from shame or regrets of the past, and forgive others to move forward together.

DARE TO BE TRUE. Be true to who you are by being your authentic self. Be seen, really seen, as to who you are rather than personifying others. After all, they are already taken.

DARE TO COMFORT. Share kind, empathetic words and warm, caring hugs. Be a rainbow in somebody else's cloud.

DARE TO STOP NEGATIVE THOUGHTS. If you catch yourself having a negative thought like, "I'm terrible at building new relationships," reframe that thought more productively like, "I find building new relationships challenging, but I continue to work at it, and I'm improving."

DARE TO FIND BALANCE. Balance in work and life isn't something you find; it is something you consciously create and work really hard to maintain.

DARE TO BE DISCIPLINED. Discipline is the bridge between goals and accomplishment. Walk across the bridge from what you want now to what you want more.

DARE TO BE ACCOUNTABLE. Acknowledge your role in difficult situations, no matter how unpleasant or unfair the situations may appear to be. Admit mistakes you own and consider if/how you can fix them.

DARE TO BE CONFIDENT. Confidence comes when you stop comparing yourself to others, understand your limitations, and love the person you are. Confidence is the new "sexy."

DARE TO BE SUCCESSFUL. Go after the success you desire with all your heart and soul. Don't sit back and wait for things to happen; make them happen yourself.

DARE TO NOT JUDGE. Behind every person is a reason why they are the way they are. Judging doesn't help; compassion does.

DARE TO CHANGE. If you continue to do what you always did, you'll always get what you've always got. So choose to make your life better with change, rather than hoping it gets better by chance.

DARE TO CELEBRATE. Applaud your accomplishment by treating yourself to a favorite pastime, hobby or appropriate indulgence. You deserve it!

No matter where you go and what you decide to do in life, dare to live fully. Every day, awake and make small daily enhancements, which over time, lead to transformative results. Choose to follow *The One Choice Rule* and dare to be your best you.

"With each sunrise there's a brand new start,
So breathe in deeply and follow your heart.
Take the chance and make the choice,
To dare to live life fully, with meaning and voice."

Tracy Butz

Personal Challenge

Are your choices leading you in the direction toward living your best life?

If you want to live a fuller, more purposeful and meaningful life, change must follow. What daily enhancements will you make to produce transformative results?

Final Thought

You know you want to be the person you were made to be. But, your time, heart and energy may have been sucked dry by guilt, distractions, and not knowing where to go next. As I promised in the introduction, you just discovered 10 powerful paver stones you can use to create the path for transforming your life. This choice lies with you.

Remember to continue to strive to be a better you without flawlessness. Display trust and confidence in your decisions. Develop habits with positive ripple effects. Replace unwanted behaviors with optimistic alternatives. Believe you are worthy to achieve success. Commit to being more courageous without regret. Demonstrate strength and resilience when facing tough times. Alter interpretations to impact your outcomes. Strive to influence thoughts and behavior change in others. And challenge yourself to live your life with purpose and meaning.

My hope is that I have influenced and inspired you to make the changes you want to make in your life, as well as those you know you should make. The One Choice Rule: *One choice can change everything.*

About the Author

TRACY BUTZ is the infusion of an engaging, powerful and poignant speaker, who masterfully influences positive behavior change. Whether she is sharing a message with 7, 70 or 700+, audiences can be found sitting on the edge of their seats, laughing aloud and brushing away tears.

Tracy proudly holds the designation of Certified Speaking Professional® (CSP), which is the highest honor in her profession, held by only 12% of speakers worldwide. She also brings more than 20 years of speaking experience from both large- and small-size clients including the US Army, Motorola, Shopko, US Bank and Subway, to name a few.

With a genuine passion for writing, Tracy became a prolific and accomplished best-selling author, with her fifth book released in early 2019. As a speaker of choice, Tracy is enthusiastic and committed to help you live a more passionate, productive and purposeful life. When looking for a dynamic speaker who understands client's needs, delivers on her promises, and drives energy and success to your event, Tracy Butz is your solution.

TracyButz.com
920.450.2118
tracy@tracybutz.com

How Can You Use This Book?

Motivate

Educate

Thank

Inspire

Promote

Connect

Why have a personalized version of *The One Choice Rule?*

- Build stronger personal bonds with family, friends, customers, prospects, colleagues and employees.

- Develop a long-lasting reminder of your event, milestone or celebration.

- Provide a keepsake that inspires change in behavior and leads to an enhanced life.

- Deliver the ultimate thank you gift that remains on coffee tables and bookshelves.

Books are thoughtful gifts that provide a genuine sentiment. They promote employee discussions and interaction, reinforce an event's meaning, and make a lasting impression. Gift this book and the #1 hand stress reliever—a fun way to say thank you and show how much you care.

More Books Authored by Tracy

HOLY COW! How to Create an Amazing Workplace that Steers Passion, Performance & Prosperity

The Perfect Pair of Jeans: Design Your Life to Fit You Dream It. Plan It. Live It.

Tame the Turbulence! Avoid Losing It. Fly Through It. 10 Maneuvers to Stop Stress from Spiraling Out of Control

Conscious Choices: 10 Powerful Strategies to Grab Control and Transform Your Life

Books can be purchased at:
TracyButz.com